THE SPOILS

COPYRIGHT © 2009 Ted Mathys
COVER & BOOK DESIGN Linda S. Koutsky
AUTHOR PHOTOGRAPH © Aram Jibilian

Coffee House Press books are available to the trade through our primary distributor, Consortium Book Sales & Distribution, www.cbsd.com or (800) 283-3572. For personal orders, catalogs, or other information, write to: info@coffeehousepress.org.

Coffee House Press is a nonprofit literary publishing house. Support from private foundations, corporate giving programs, government programs, and generous individuals help make the publication of our books possible. We gratefully acknowledge their support in detail in the back of this book.

Good books are brewing at coffeehousepress.org

LIBRARY OF CONGRESS CATALOGING-IN-PUBLICATION DATA
Mathys, Ted, 1979–
The spoils / Ted Mathys.
p. cm.
ISBN 978-1-56689-230-8 (alk. paper)
I. Title.
PS3613.A829S66 2009
811'.6—DC22
2008052609

FIRST EDITION | FIRST PRINTING
1 3 5 7 9 8 6 4 2
Printed in the United States

ACKNOWLEDGMENTS

Some of these poems, in earlier incarnations, have appeared in *American Poetry Review, BOMB, Conjunctions, Fence, jubilat, KGB Bar Lit,* and *Puppy Flowers.* Thanks to the editors of these publications. "The New Atlas" appeared in the exhibition *Earth on Stone on Earth is Naturally So* at Flashpoint Gallery, Washington, DC.

My gratitude goes to the following poets and artists, whose ideas, comments, and verve were instrumental to the writing of this book: Karl Krause, Ben Lerner, Nick Rattner, Fred Schmalz, Sophie Smith, Chris Stackhouse, and Kendra Sullivan. For his singular graciousness and curiosity, I am grateful to Chris Martin. Thanks also to Chris Fischbach and the staff at Coffee House Press for their energy and dedication. Thank you Greg Hewett, for friendship that is "not an idle sympathy and mutual consolation merely, but a heroic sympathy of aspiration and endeavor."

for Rachel Smith

CONTENTS

A SOCCER BALL FOR DR. KISSINGER

THE SPOILS

A SOCCER BALL
FOR DR. KISSINGER

4 weeks. A dozen stadia. 32 squads. 72,000 square meters of turf. Flamelets green. Ganglion roots.

Divots under cleats. Legs in kinesis. Cadence of quadriceps. 32 panels. Synthetic leather. 20 white hexagons.

Thermally molded. 12 dark pentagons. Ideally placed. 5-ply twisted polyester thread. Structure & bounce.

Airborne. Aerial slice. Magnus force. State of nature. Ideation. Truncated icosahedron. Spindrift of bullets.

4 forwards. Flash tactic. 4 midfielders. Operating in anarchy. Syndicated pixel. Sweat-heavy jerseys.

Momentary sarabande. 2 defenders. Skills analogous to ballet. Stitched or glued. Juggled on kneecaps. Butyl

bladder. Skills analogous to foot drill. Ricochet. Punctum. Radii out from the center. Constituting the posited

limits. Spherical. The clarity of *victor*. Running out the clock. Rounders. Eyeballs. Clarity of the L column.

Testicle as failed sphere. Venn diagram handed over to stillness. Versus vs. Versus. Photon launched from

dim peripheral star. Parasphere. Telstar. Tango. Conflict the periodic fluke of peace. Ideals vs. Interests.

Photon entering the retinal rod. Superstar. The stadium's standing O. Dislodging an opsin protein. The will

to see. Peace the periodic fluke of conflict. Tango Durlast. Earth in profile. Identical from all angles.

Delivery system. Tango España. The spindrift of bullets. Arc of the foot. The O in One. Azteca. Etrusco.

Strike of the striker's shoe. Glide. Gnarled fists. Questra. Embryo. Degree zero. Shot at the net. Cranial emergence. The O in zero. Payload. *Beautifully and illegally.* Fevernova. Tricolore. Icon. Geist.

SPHERE OF INFLUENCE

Not infrequently in the collected tales of good and evil, we have transgressed ourselves directly into storks. For pissing off some facile deity or other, we are punished into blowfish, or concealed in a cryptocrystalline chunk of agate, or in the river striving over it, or in the knotted tree reflected in the current, or, most commonly, retrofitted with the mesothorax of a hideous insect. Careful where you walk, a chapter says, careful where you rest your teeth;

On the verso, as if to show the geological is equally at the disposal of indiscriminate authority, mountains and canyons and stands of timber, too, have been muzzled into human form, a special kind of spatial hell. You yourself contain gorges more flush and violent, a chapter says, faces steeper and edges sharper, a chapter says, than you could possibly know;

After spectacles of punishment come tales of *coming to,* dumbly bumping into critical scenarios. In the margin between saying and said you find yourself in a dark wood, ready to descend, or you wake with a mouthful of pebbles, blackjacked in the good eye from an unknown source;

Bearing no elephantiasis or antennae, in no foreign clutch of oaks, I came to on Madison Avenue, anchored in acres of familiar masonry. Ejected from the opulent lobby through the *whump, whump* of revolving doors into the steady entropy of the week. Past scrunches of gardenias at the bodega, as always; past the mosaic of a maniacal lion at the library extension, as always. This throat is familiarly mine, I thought, these hands. Through an atrium full of bamboo, past a statue of a cadmium yellow bugle all knotted up to skunk the harmonium. This necktie, ditto, these shoes, ditto, this gait;

I combed the index of the collected tales of good and evil for the passage where a sly transformation exists in which no catastrophic change is necessary to make all that was foreign familiar, all that is now familiar into the body's foreign, phantom limb. Through security, swallowed by an elevator, up to reception and insufferable pleasantries, as little diplomat or foreign policy flunkie, I was tasked to deliver an official World Cup game ball to Kissinger, a gift from one aging statesman to another, signed with a Sharpie, *Lieber Henry . . .*

The question is not how the credulous goat got where he got, a chapter says, it's what he does once there, a chapter says. To punt in protest off into the fountain is a waste of leg. To play the role of dutiful messenger opposed to his message is the history of the twentieth century. To punt in protest is at least to see their virtual handshake spin and disappear into turbulence. To deliver the gift is both an act and actless, like torching one's self on the Capitol steps. I tossed the sphere back and forth. They shook and unshook and shook.

Lieber Henry, you were supposed to be

metonymy for evil, a conceptual public mensch
in possession of a ghastly seventies haircut
and bulletproof eyes, not a squat
body standing within body
heat of me beyond the chancery beyond
the waft of odorous July
asphalt in the capital, caught with the rest of us
in the crosshairs of the polar
symmetry of the reception hall
at the ambassador's residence,
regarding the architectural leitmotif of square
upon clinical square upon
which cocktails and cross-cultural interaction
play out like game theory
on an imperfect grid, your pressed monkey suit
every bit as banal and ahistorical
as mine. You were supposed to wield
a snifter of cognac and a cigar or slambo
shots of Jäger in honor of your native
Fürth, not nurse
a glass of water and with
solemnity analyze the tripartite
balance of power forming between a wizened
carrot, a gherkin, and a gob of ranch dip
on your buffet plate. The open bar opens
onto a terrace of journalists

picking at jerk chicken & yammering about ag
policy and the tyranny of subsidies,
opens onto a four-tiered lawn bombed with magnolias
stepping down to a reflecting pool
chock full of tangerine sky. Public policy surfaces
from the accumulated perturbations
of private psychological histories
and private insecurities are predicated
in no small part upon the unforgiving
parameters of public norms
so what could it possibly mean
for both of us to be swatting with resolve
at the same damn cabbage moth
white and erratic as popcorn on a string
as it bounces up the lawn? A leveling? An end
to the logic of ambition? No more
than the incongruous protocols of *official*
and *natural?* You were supposed to sit
on too many boards to have shown
up at a function routine
as this, let alone piss in the same
public men's room in the residence
as the rest of the ambassador's guests.
From across the marble partition
I listen to your tusk of urine
spear the water in the bowl
as I run a tusk of water over my palms
in the sink. The photo of you on the wall
dribbling a soccer ball past a humoring
Beckenbauer anticipates the stance

you strike as you emerge
from the privacy of the stall
like a mass of thawing clay, approach the soap
dispenser, nod, drone
in your sonorous voice *Good evening*.
Contained for a moment within my wingspan
is intimate circumstance made in an instant
public, historical, worldwide. I boil, clench, lunge

and respond *Good evening* in kind.

TWELVE FUNDAMENTALS

First there is what matters.
Once it matters it is measured.
Measured as mass.
Mass is the amount of matter in an object.
For example, in a rifle.
In relations of matter and mass,
celestial location is inconsequential.
A rifle in the spheres is a rifle in Akron.

     Second,

distinguished from mass,
weight is the tug of gravity
on a given rifle, polished or no.
The gun, then, bears heavier on the man
who carries it through Akron than on the man
who drifts with it on his fingertips
through the spindle of planetary spheres.
This distinction between the weapon's
mass and weight must be maintained
to prevent the properties
by which we live from being
blown to rags.

     Third,

to further pickle and preserve the balances
by which we live, a truly stellar man

must, then, refuse to entertain
how the gravity of his decisions
play out in Akron.

Fourth,

gravity is one fashion of force.
A force causes a body to change
in speed or direction. As in, slammed
limp and laterally across the narthex
by a seismic quake or fragmentation grenade.
This is what we mean by *influence*.
In Akron, then, when any man
influenced by conscience or conscription
slings his rifle from his shoulder meat
toward the great metallic lake to the north,
a force causes it to make for the very
center of what we call Earth.

Fifth,

hard work is an American virtue.
Work is done when a force moves
an object in the direction of that force.
For example, gravity or gunpowder
pulling a flock of swifts or a round
with their beak dive or its spindrift
down into a chimney or a sternum.

Sixth,

the amount of hard work achieved
is the product of the distance
that the bird or the round travels
and the force acting upon it — in this instance,
gravity or infantry offensive.
Merely applying force to an object
is not scored as honest work
unless measurable motion takes place.
For example, a semicircle of radicals
sedentary on private property in middle Akron
taking baton blows to collarbones
amid swifts funneling overhead
is doing absolutely no hard work.
If, however, the collaborative forces
of batons plus plummeting birds
causes the collective of radicals to collect
their plum-lovely injuries and flee,
some serious work is getting done.

Seventh,

the rate at which work gets done
is called *power*. Power is the amount
of work chalked up per unit of time.
For instance, measured in terms
of splash, the rifle slung in Akron is long
enough airborne en route
toward the great metallic lake to the north

and is pulled down forcefully enough
toward the Earth's loin pit — where in
the heat its chamber
and hammer will melt
to dross — to be
powerful as hell.

    Eighth,

time, here, is the kicker.
The ambitious mission of man is to assure
with his flawless delivery and deadfinger salute
to the arena flashing like plankton
that the present is not the matter, is prologue,
that the future is secure, that there always *will be*
another Akron in which we *will live*
better. This is what we mean by politics.

    Ninth,

in politics power is the capacity
to change the behavior of others
to get the outcomes one wants.
But in order to measure changed behavior
the preferences of the others must be known.
For example, when a man in Akron
is told to "swallow this barrel,
motherfucker," we must be sure
he does not already prefer
to swallow this barrel, motherfucker.
Otherwise power is an illusion.

Tenth,

the crux of politics is prolix:
power sketched out in the excess of languages.
The rest of politics is proxemics:
allegiance to the authority of official distances
between conceptual artillery and actual arteries.

Eleventh,

as in Akron, in the lightless spheres
the once and comfy notion of absoluteness
has been outed over time as tyrannical.
Replaced by situational, amorphous morals.
Spiring irony: absent absolute
all becomes permissible;
orgiastic confetti of cartridges,
sprinkles on the whitest of ice cream.

Thus, to last,

the man on the ground never abandons
his rusty-ass Akron. He must imagine
a resistance unknown
to conceptual circles, position himself
vis-à-vis the wordless
vacuity of worlds without gravity,
must walk train tracks for answers
and never look up.

Thus, to last,

the man adrift in the spheres
remains rootless, maintains the essential
elements of his arsenal. He must believe
Akron is as Akron is
and was and will always be,
and violence is violence and war
is war and in order to maintain order
over pile upon pile of *my dead body*
one must do what one must do.
For when in doubt, tautology.
This is what we mean
by *crisis of imagination.*

Ticket. Turnstile. Lucky stub. Follow the floodlight. Warm-ups. Single file. Counterfeit. Rookie dribble.

Monkey roll. Quick sprint. Hawk scheme. Condiment. Emissaries in the glass box. Ticket. Counterfeit.

Back channel. Face paint. Oversold. Six deep in stairwell. Shin guard. Scalp fat. Indigo torsos. Serifs

stitched white. Maxing out seatbacks. On laps. Piggy backed. Peering from railings. From latrines. Rung

straddle. Scaling pylons. Edging the pitch. Emissaries stovepiping the paperchoke. The huddle. The whistle.

The kick. Mass impulse. No locus. Slide tackle. No clear direction or purpose. Header. Endocrines in

synchrony. Steel fencing. Solid. Jostle for aisle. Sudden like the devil's hooves up the spine. Floodlit rumpled

animal in cloud cover. Pure empyrean surge. A forearm jammed into rubbish bin. Flight of stairs.

Flight of bottles. The tallest succumb. Seatback discus. Leg twisted up purple like a pipe cleaner. Emissary

gasping in the glass box. National whirlpool. Team scatter. Teeming tunnel. Onset of hypoxia. Black helmets.

Deadbolted exit. Goalpost canted in the rush. Face into nape. Dioxide rising. Blue hair, blue jersey, blue.

Handrail into sailor knots. No arterial oxygen diffusion. 4500 Newtons. Waver optic. Horizontal force.

Working paper. Anaerobic metabolism. *Our last offer.* Lactic acid. Abstract emissary signature. Tendon burn.

Total anoxia. Dough through a sieve. Palms on glass. Floodlight plundering heaven for a glory hole. Shooting through. Technically a draw. A minute of silence. More common than an earthquake. Stricken from the record.

A CUT IN THE OFFING

Meaning

A slice is coming

Implying

Injury in the future

Reiterate

A cut in the offing

For once

Reduction is imminent

Implying

Slews will come home

Forswear

A cut in the offing

Stipulate

Fewer go off

Meaning

Fewer are offed

Entailing

A curb in the carnage

(Cut that)

A cut in the killing

Suggesting

Incisions in bodies

Consider it

A cut in the offing

Requiring

A wound in the making

Meaning

Making is suffering

For once

A cut in the offing

Is

A slash in the future

Meaning

The future is vulnerable

Meaning

Show me your hands

Lieber Henry, I am considering our time

together in Rio, how up through the cipher
of citizens and avenues we rose
in a cog train, Corcovado's
cragged granite vocabulary translated by rack
and pinion into postindustrial
rattle between our shoes, how the car —
relieved for the occasion of its burden
to negotiate ecological constraints
on behalf of human ambition in multiple —
opened onto an urban forest
gagged with clouds, how during the ride
you coolly autopsied an avocado
and ate the soft slices off
the back of your knife,
how from the terminus we hiked
through a fine, polluted mist
to the foot of twelve
hundred tons of concrete redemption,
Cristo Redentor spreading his well-
carved hands without traditional
diplomatic aplomb, south with right,
north with left, Christ's huge chest
pointing ahead in the direction of the world's
largest soccer stadium, how my desire
to understand was born on a mountaintop
from a desire to be
you at that altitude and a desire to know

the sound a screwdriver might make
gliding through your throat,
how before we left
the heavy toes of eschatology
for the stadiums of modernity, I leaned
over the railing and dropped your name
into the dark and noiseless lake of decades
below, how it entered
without fanfare but sent
ripples for miles, how we waited
together for them to reach an edge, a bank,
a consequence, some manner of tangible cattail
or lily pad, how instead
what was displaced continues to expand
hourly in imperceptible swells,
how watching them move
was watching the stadium do
The Wave in perpetuity, how watching them
move I wanted to tell you that I, too,
embrace a certain form of radical
practicality — for instance, the first
time I took down an elk,
before the roast, we filled the chainsaw
with vegetable oil in order

to carve without tainting the meat.

THE NATIONAL INTEREST

We are interested in long criminal histories
because we've never bedded down in a cellblock.
With the sibilance of wind through the swaying
spires of skyscrapers as my witness. When I say
cover your grenades I mean it's going to rain I mean
there is mischief in every filibuster of sun.

We are interested in rigorously arranging
emotions by color as we've never been fully
divested of blues. With drinking till my fingernails
hurt as my witness, with hurt as my witness.
When I say be demanding I mean be fully
individual while dissolving in the crowd.

We are interested in characters who murder
because we've never committed it or to it.
With an origami frog in a vellum crown spinning
on a fishing line from the ceiling as my witness.
When I say please kneel with me I mean between
every shadow and sad lack falls a word.

We are interested in ceaselessly setting floor joists
because we've never pulled a pole barn spike
from a foot. With bowing to soap your ankles
in the shower as my witness, lather as my witness.
When I say did you see the freckle in her iris I mean
the poem must reclaim the nature of surveillance.

We are interested in possessing others who possess
that which we possess but fear losing in the future.
With a fork as my witness. A dollop of ketchup,
hash brown, motion, with teeth as my witness.
When I say you I don't mean me I don't mean
an exact you I mean a composite you I mean God.

We are interested in God because we can't
possess God, because we can't possess *you*.
With a scrum of meatheads in Izod ogling iPods
as my witness, technological progress as my witness.
When I say no such thing as progress in art I mean
"These fragments I have shored against my ruins."

We are interested in ambivalence as ribcages
resist being down when down, up when up.
With the swell of the argument and the moment
before forgiveness as my witness. When I say power
is exclusion I mean a box of rocks we don't
desire to deduce I mean knowing is never enough.

Carabiners with screw gates. Ripped tees & trunks. Headlamp ready in *the other theater*. Hoard your socks.

Earth is a turtle. Speleological hoopla. The shell is a mount. Mud and mulberry along the river to the karst.

The cave is a mouth. Passport stamps bleeding in the leaky dry bag. Countries mashed indiscriminately together by water. Shitloads of DEET. Jocular commodore above the sampan. Helmets. Each headlamp an

oculus. Doggy paddle into mouth. Reverse Orpheus. The mouth a voyeuristic eye, following what it speaks.

Limestone protrusions. Gauge the overbearing. Frigid at nipples. *Where 800 lived.* Clay underfoot. Bat pits

like postholes. Dug with eons of spit. Reenactment: flaming paper battleship floated into dark. Diminution of the orb. 1,600 eyes rising like bubbles through black water. Surfacing as the battleship passes. Sinking

back into heads. Finding bodies. Hauling themselves out. Reclaiming reinforced natural doorways. Bunker.

Blockhouse. Pillbox. Calcite stalactite busted up for lintels. Countersunk in mud. Turtle gut. Eating Area.

Hygiene Area. Sleeping shelf. Rations under padlock. 60 flintlock rifles propped. Antiaircraft pom pom

webbed with rust. Generator groan. The seep of herbicides and defoliants. Raven pilots over the mountain.

8 years underground. Votive to the last. Ravens in blue jeans. Ravens with dark tans. 1.9 metric tons of

ordnance. Wayward soccer ball into Unsanitary Area. 4 meters of drop. 3 weeks of feces. Raven blast.

Punish the goalie. Flashlights turned on his chest. His neck swarmed by insects. Followed by the bats.

STATUTE OF LIMITATIONS

Octogenarian jedermann statesman
passed forth & forth through his later years
on public hands & faces must
dwell there beneath strobe and lave
hidden from him in macular
failure, brink light, din. Swell
and rise in eddying arms, a shoelace
aflutter in the roil. What corporal
cloud need sacrifice its particulars
in order to pass this body on
& on, an operative clause
toward the riderless horse in trot
behind the caisson pulling his casket
through a vale of public buildings
draped in bunting? Zinc taste
hard in his mouth and stomach signal
the coming gun carriage, honor guard,
missing man formation in the jets
overhead, suspension of the stocks,
the courts, the mail, a convoy
of limousines, a ban on fishing,
to lie in state beneath the dome,
to stomach the howitzer's guttural
thunk, hand on heart, doff the hat,
half-mast, the bugler, taps.

*

Until then, augury must do.
A gavel in Parliament snaps,
the first portent. The former potentate
surrounds himself with dwarves and lines
his pockets with red jasper spirit
stones fresh from the tumbler.
The plane of all reverence
may stroke the albino buffalo's
global rump for luck and lush crops
but no manner of animist ritual
will release him from the story of hands
because nature has signaled
it is not yet ready to receive him.
The faults slip a minor quake,
a mudslide assumes his birthplace
and sky over the national airport
where the coronation was performed
is a wrung sponge. Continual discontent
with the height of the table he lies on
to exorcise. Power has an essence
all its own, it goes, and the flaming womb
is indifferent to the diffidence of age.
Not before the shades of his rule
are cleansed, it goes, will he
be handed the blood red amaryllis,
golden pollen fallen from its anthers
whirling, blown to twilight.

*

There is a statute of limitations on rage
and it's no longer true *the evil men do*
lives after them while *the good is oft*
interred with their bones.
Modern medicine declares
a war of attrition and elderly statesmen
learn to outlive their actions.
In senescence his body is twice
divided, once from former vigor, once
from the torus of events themselves.
Palms now toss in a whorl about
an empty center, trying to orient
themselves to a neighbor, but history
has become the simple procedure
by which the previous becomes beyond
moral reproach. With no other recourse
we invite him to pause from
obligatory revisionist memoirs
to weigh in on the flair and passing
skills of the Italian soccer team
or deliver, at our endless gala dinner,
the honorary keynote on the topic of honor.

*

You have felt him in the titanium
driver's sweet spot connecting
with a golf ball, in the topspin
& soft white effort disappearing
over the fairway. He has flashed
you a quiet, catenary smile

through a cable on the bridge
& drawn a meteor across your late
slate sky, the lesson's thick chalk
in its wake. You have seen
the arc of his oratory in sparklers
lobbed by a boy into the reservoir
each night, in flowers raining
into a bull ring. You have found him
here, watching from the upper tier
as the torero passes a cape in flirtation
telling the story of dominance
in a spectacle of dust. A false theater
in which real death occurs, picadors
bouncing on horses & banderillas
drawing ribbons from the flanks.
It is the very frivolity of the kill
that makes the spectator human
for if the final sword were a necessity
for food or hide or horn
the courage & knowledge of man
would still overwhelm
the strength & ignorance of the bull,
but there'd be no such thing as style
and death could not be beautiful.

*

Always at dawn, always with juniper
incense smoldering in the margins.
On an elevated platform
on a windswept steppe

the body is readied by monks
for summoned scavenger birds.
Or always at night, always with cigarette
lighters waving in synchrony
over a platform of hands.
He floats on the crowd like a pro,
occluding our encore
in a quick eclipse. A kettle of vultures
can disperse through nations the bits
on disinterested wings, but in concert
the statesman temporizes, cloven
only by self from self & we are
impelled to deliver him
to a balcony to address the press
gaggle assembled below.
Pleasure is in his body falling
into word & ink & word offset
lithographic in newsprint,
dissolving into coverage, fanning
wide over the subscriber base
as he walks away from the stadium,
apotheosis of a living ghost.
In the rhythmic click of wing tips
on marble, complexities are compressed
into space constraints by editors fluent
in headlinese. Prohibit becomes ban,
abolish becomes axe, negotiations
are talks, the victim count is a toll,
to arrest is to nab, attack is assail,
and universal convention
is to omit the verb *to be*.

Lieber Henry, I clobber calories on a hamster wheel

as you are interviewed by a colorless rose.
In pixels you float in mute a foot
in front of my huff,
run through your final hunches and hackles,
addle a fold in the napkin on the dais
as the public access camera rolls.
Our best machines adjust successes
for variations in age, complicity, and weight.
From 7 mph I up to 8. Needlework of sweat
corners the eyes while a wall of mirrors
before us assures all pain is public.
To your theoretical left a woman pumps
with rigor her angled arms, watches a docudrama
on an emergency surgery on a pasty marine's
caved-in chest, ascends
her endless stairs to a nowhere
it took us ages to create.
Our best machines adjust successes
for variations in the volume of blood
flooding the shunts of the modern heart.
On screen the rose gleams
in its glass of tap water
in the center of a worn wing chair
opposite you in the studio shorn of ornament
and temporality, vacuumed of all light
except, of course, for the scorching, deific spot.

The flower has been posed as if to pose
the opening question, which turns out to be
no question. You fidget and sip.
I up to 8.2. Again the rose refuses
and again. Redact the red of broken capillaries
and love; redact the white of tidal breakers
and surrender; redact the yellow of friendship
and cowardice, this flower is colorless,
unobstructed by those frivolous values
threatening as ever its resource constraints.
You slide your paw through your ashen hair.
I spit on my mini towel. With no question,
no conflict. With no conflict, you possess
no message, glower instead
at your passive interlocutor and commence
mouthing inaudible responses. I up to 8.8.
The studio's blackness becomes you,
preventing the silence in your tumbling gestures,
in your impatient lips, in the bowtie
toggling your throat from being
heard as the sum
total of a life's events.
I once dunked a near-flat
soccer ball but had to travel
egregiously to do it. The theory of the game
collapses once you're informed
that all this time you've been playing
the wrong game.
Given gesture, given silence
I am forced to foist upon you my own

pathetic extended exchange.
No language to gauge the logic of continual
conditioning amid sedentary conditions.
Above you our best machines
double in a wall of mirrors, and we are

running toward ourselves as fast as we can.

After aggression. Cushion pass. Absolado. Iced ankle. After penalties of adrenaline. All fans banned from the stadium. Clean carom. Mundial. Vencida. After volunteer sorters. Copa. Tunit. After terminal moraine.

Purple unidentifieds. Faint click. Leather to leather. Insole to ball. After legislation. No flag. No slogan.

No anthem. Polyvalent white nugget of phosphor. The O in iota. Cat's cradle of vectors down an expansive

green palm. Subtle grunt. Exertion huff. After the cordon. After the barricade. No applause. No face paint.

No faces. Passed & passed. Match play. Coaches, journalists, police. The phosphorescence of emptiness.

Captain bark. Strategy pinging like rubber bullets. No hothead. No bellyful. Wicker light. Lung butter against the dew point. Ref whistle in a vacuum. Goal. No cataclysm. No announcer. Another. No showboat. Unstable

geometries. Heel to heel over whose green palm. No uproar. The *ono* of testicles in iconoclast. Formulas

sweeping a curtain of uniformed men. Formosa. Traction. Toward the shredded celadon sea. Removable

soleplate for inclement conditions. Tightened with a stud key. Humans assigned a number & color. The field

a kinetic green pupil. Deified athletes skittering in the vitreous hole. Mobile white node over blades. Black

pupil in white ball in green pupil in radial concrete iris. Audible breath. Removable soleplate. Fans held *en*

masse beyond the barricade. Whole electorate of cataracts. In the frontier of sclera. Radios clutched. Red

card. Contagious applause in the saline perimeter. Under the lid of night. Insole. Insole. Kilometers away.

THE SPOILS

ADAPTATION

It was not in my nature to prefer progress on principle.
Nor was it in my nature to oppose to the artificial
ficus in the optometrist's office a dogwood in wilderness
dropping a solitary blossom into a pool of koi,
for that, neither, was ever in my nature. My nature
was unknown to me, but hi-def nature shows
were growing on me, flash frozen Alaskan salmon
was growing on me, and MapQuest, and happy hour,
and water bottled at the source. It was not in my nature
to ascribe purity to the past. Nostalgia a wasted emotion,
waste an ecological concern. Tomatoes in December
were growing on me, a vine of them garlanding my neck.
Adaptation was in my nature, so I grew inured to this.
The par five on the back nine with a dogleg left
at the clubhouse was growing on me. And oven cleaner,
a 24-hour call center, free checking appended to my chest.
My safety was growing on me. I was so safe
I could scarcely breathe. Boneless skinless bloodless
chicken breasts metastasized over my thighs like scales.
Gas logs, the derivatives market, surround sound
and L.L. Bean catalogues were growing on me.
Though I had grown immobile and unable to see,
this was in my nature. I was an ecology.

FIRST LIGHT

Believing

        as she has evolved

        over many millennia

                to believe

that the brightest light

        at midnight belongs

                to the clang of the moon

                on the black ocean glass

      the loggerhead

          turtle hatchling

              follows her instinct

              for a luminous source

         a carapace writing

         a line in the sand

flipper over

      flipper toward

           the Wal-Mart

           parking lot.

GAME PLAN FOR WESTERN MAN

Let's say in the snowball Earth scenario
only forty-one percent of all readers prefer
a happy ending. Or let's say metalepsis is total, Ohio

gains on Iceland, effect humps cause, Maine defers
to Iranian lobsters and Congressional spouses
are coached to speak only in non sequiturs.

When state birds fled the states that espoused
their colors and causes, I took up melting circuit boards
in a wok to fish out microchips and arouse

myself with flecks of gold. According
to The Internet, despite voluminous transboundary
movement of e-waste my kid still can't afford

gold teeth. For pork buns he solders lead patiently
over a hot plate lent to us by the dude sluicing
microchips in an acid bath. In the new economy

you'll find me at ebb tide's edge, chewing on dulse.
The percentage of readers who can stomach more violent
endings correlates negatively with age. To traduce

the logic of exuberant growth, we spent
nights with s'mores and a bonfire of electrical wires,
aluminum revealed by melting plastic in the main event.

Swing a hammer, fat lady, at the old glass monitor
to mine its copper yoke. Never say *privatization*
say *personalization*. Never say *murder*

say *sacrifice*. Let's say there's no relation
between error and second chance. Then a cape of Tyvek
flapping from a dormer in rain was aesthetic perfection.

My dog got addicted to hallucinogenic toads so I got drunk
and fucked your superdelegate. Latex gloves
and resuscitation masks are available in the back.

Just keep doing what you're doing.
I will tell you when to stop.

THE DISCIPLINE OF SNOWFLAKES

All snowmen
in Brooklyn
    have plastic forks for arms
        and suffer the public
        opprobrium of being

    eleven inches tall
      fronting the bile
  of Gowanus Canal

from sleet-wet
    front stoops,
    the predicate of desire
        to witness the collective
        corpus subjected
        to the elemental joke

and reflected,
    however
    pathetically,
    however
in miniature,
        in an irrepressible
        event of nature,

except for those who've outgrown
their fallen ontic realm,

are human-high
and exactly one

in number, at the foot of a slow
white declivity in the Nethermead,
surrounded

by a ring of boys,
each with a five-gallon bucket
as pediment,
pissing on the snowman's head.

In the science of imaginary solutions
I only make camp
with blind men

warming their hands
at an invisible fire.

Each of them has seen the seagull

loosed from his screech
coursing through a flurry
feeling nothing
of terrestrial borders
as the land beneath him

becomes sand, and the sand
water, the water
deeper

                              as the tidal shelf slopes away

and temperature
              decreases, pressure
increases, light
                    dims as day
                    and night strike
                                        a note of irrelevance, krill, bits

       of microscopic decomposed organic
       matter and irreducible
                              plastic polymers

              drift down peaceably,
              deep marine snow.

DOWN DINKY BANK TO COAL HOLE DOWN DINKY BANK
TO COAL WHAT SEEMS AT FIRST ARE SEAMS AT
BLACK MARIA BLACK AT FIRST IN THIRTY MINUTES
THE LANDSCAPE CHANGES IN THIRTY MINUTES THE
LANDSCAPE MARIA OPEN CAST LIGNITE BELLY OPEN
CAST LIGNITE CHANGES SCRAPING AWAY AT THE
EARTH SCRAPING AWAY AT THE BELLY ONE HUNDRED
TONS OF ROSEBUD PER DAY ONE HUNDRED TONS OF
ROSEBUD PER EARTH MAKE YOUR HOME ON A BLACK
VEIN MAKE YOUR HOME ON A BLACK DAY EMINENT
DOMAIN EMINENT VEIN CHAIN YOUR WAIST TO A
TRUNK CHAIN YOUR WAIST TO A DOMAIN RIPCORD ON
THE CHAINSAW RIPCORD ON THE TRUNK LIFT YOUR
DAMN LEGS GRANOLA HEAD I DON'T WANT TO CUT OFF
YOUR FEET

THE FREQUENCIES

Pouring a cylindrical blue

                   container of table salt

                   into a shaker

                                 the hand dissolves

into the hiss of sand

               peeled off a dune

                        by the wind of rearrangement

                       across the desert

and the geometry of laughter

                   between the walls

                   of a titanic shopping mall

rising from the bronze terrain
where under fluorescence

                  families pay by the hour

                            for downhill skiing

                            on refrigerated snow.

SIX PACK AND AXE

Shiners flit below this window

                in ice, in and out

                of the plastic rings of

                          a Diet Coke

                          six pack yoke

          suspended in water

                limpid

                as a diamond.

                Below

the halo of bubbles

        the head of an axe

        is sunk in mud

                      where it has been hidden

                      since a man

exhausted by his age

        fled to the woods to fish

                      for pickerel through a hole

              in time,

              and feeling finished

      in every sense

      stood at the edge

                looking off into shrub oaks

                                                    and pitch pines
                                                    girdled in snow

and tossed his axe behind his back
                              where it slid four rods
                              across the ice, disappeared

into the hole,
descended,
its helve erect,
                    to the bed,
                    where it stood
                    for nothing, for the better
                                        part of a century

as the handle rotted off
                    before my very eyes
                    arrived.

EVENING RIVEN

to run toward
burning leaves
evening riven

yam sky up
to wall of slate
clouds, clean

division broken
by roots of rain
trailing deep

double horizon
without a name
to speak like this

smell in
air = taste
in water

Portuguese
man-o-war
full of nitrogen

secreted by gland
floated by wind
on ocean surface

clean division
broken by high
voltage tentacles

studded with toxins
trailing deep
below horizon

single species
of fish immune
without a name

to dart inscrutable
among the nettles
to nibble poison

bit by bit
to run toward
burning leaves

gamely mimic
precarious tree
in scent of worms

stroke in
water = stroke
on canvas

before an artist
as model falls
asleep on divan

clean division
broken by hand
falling from cushion

to floor as roots
of trees through soil
beyond the frame

without a name
into wide predella
as hand as rain

as root in tentacle
a sculptural violence
to think like this

but storm and growth
in arbitrary horizon
but ash from leaves

without a name
the forms are a form
of deep permission

CAPE CANAVERAL

If I concede beauty
                    is neither a pure
                    mathematical triangle
                                        scribed in the noumenal human
                                        attic of reflection

              nor a matter of what matter
                                    is actually before me

in all of its pomp
& contrariness,
                    but some arbitrary relation
                    between formal aspects

                                        of the launch pad on the horizon
                                        & the bald emotion
                                        of its phenomenally flawed critic,

                    why should it matter

the most gorgeous jellyfish
I have ever seen
                            coughed up on a beach,
              a pellucid balloon ensnared

                                        in tubular ocher kelp,

          turned out upon
                    closer inspection

                            to be a Home Depot
                            shopping bag?

69

SCENIC OVERLOOK

You have to admire the sheer

                  ambition of the clear cut

               dashing up the mountain

      circling the peak

                         just once

                         at the timber line

          and looping back on itself

               like a butterfly knot,

aspiring, at all times

         to perfect consumption,

                and as all things

                toward its own pure form:

a fully felled slope

        emptying out

           over foothills,

      a treeless delta

              into treeless plain

hardening into the flat black

         fabric of a parking lot

        where mountain goats,

        having grown

accustomed to pure

        salt taste,

        have forced

                their daft white bodies

under the fronts of mini

            vans to nurse

   on blue-green

   antifreeze.

A RESPONSE FROM INDUSTRY TO THE PROPHETS OF DOOM

All it took was a couple of prejudiced
letters from some two-desks-and-a-law-degree
outfit claiming the voice of social justice

to tip the bibliogenetic chemistry
of a reading public primed to go off quick
& half-cocked on the subject of ecology,

to liberate all the illogic, hysteria, & sophistic
nonsense of parlor pinks, Ivy League pedants,
freegans, & locavores addicted

to yoga, incipient mindlessness, & seitan,
who vie for the title of head cheerleader
in the nature rooting section

not to mention all the denser
chicken lickens of the age of unreason
who bought the asinine logomachical pressures

of these left-wing academicians
and now insist on everyone's inalienable right
to harass the police and fly the flags of this nation's

military foes, that fluttering flock of trite,
slovenly kids who with all the scientific soundness
of a voodoo rooster-plucking ceremony moan & gripe

about fertilizers, go clucking and squawking to Congress
about how we sinned against the oceans, the tilapia,
the sky, the robins, the deltas, the flowers, the grass

in a coast-to-coast outbreak of galloping myopia
to expedite the overnight ecologists' preposterous
vision of an even-steven utopia.

Never mind that detergents, while a menace
to tadpoles, were a boon to housewives, the public
had already bought the foolishness

as avidly as the buxom hausfraus of Munich
had bought the garbage of national socialism
so that cops who had simply raised a nightstick

to bop a few foul-mouthed lovers of communism
and other rock-throwing rioters
over the head were treated with awesome

scorn, even as their quasi-religious rite
of anti-chemical catharsis
essentially uncorked malaria, cholera, crop blight,

yellow fever, bubonic plague, typhus,
dengue, sleeping sickness, and dysentery
and wiped out all recourse

to ward off the flights of gnats and flies
and mosquitoes that threaten to ruin
the tradition of the backyard cookout.

RAIN IN DETROIT

Aircraft on the tarmac strut

        and suckle their jetways,

        a terminal brood at the iron

nipples of a spidery

        animal,

        control

is having a systems problem

        or the system is having

        problems with control,

                suddenly it's so

        late in the tantrum of late

capitalism that we're simply the milk.

        No longer accomplices

      of our feelings,

        everyone is becoming

a reactionary artist,

we're all painting

        the proverbial painting of rain

        lashing the tarmac

through the window's

        exclusionary frame —

Perspective demands the canvas be what it's not,
a reflection of the depth of the situation.

Abstraction permits it to be what it is, disinterested
damage stretching in ecstatic blue flatness.

Window if you do, window if you don't.

You say runways make you feel hopeless,
mistaking our painting for its emotional result.

Psychological speculation replaces criticism.
The airport disappears.

A TOTALITY FOR LEAVES

In the shape of this blankness

                    in the wake of the universal

                              leaf blower

                              issuing color

into a distant quadrant of the lawn,

                    I pool all leaflets

                    virtual and real,

            cup the entirety
of advertisements

                    in two soiled hands,

              step up a stump

                            & fling the campaigns

to the universal vacuum.
In outward distribution

                they scatter & scream

                          in the shape of autonomy

                        toward every Euclidean

        surface, assume

              facades, pages, monitors,

in a ribbon rush in

                      closing subway doors,

                            collide

                    with BlackBerries
                        and Sidekicks,

find new placement
            in the shape of the narrative,
                                smear the sweatshirts,
                                boots, the waterproof

        jackets of a sheep flock
                    in a manicured pasture
        so every ewe in Holland

                                announces Vodafone's new
                                monthly unlimited plan,

transmogrify to radio waves,

                                    skywrite in puffs,

        make new purchase
            in the shape of the mind.

THE WORLD

WERE : MAN :: *ELD* : OLD

sediment dredged from the sea bed
two kilometers off
the coast of Dubai rises
in polypropylene geotextile tubes
two meters in diameter,
sucked into carrier barges
swimming with engineers,
runs up a taut conveyor belt
and arcs in rainbows from a sand cannon
to pinpoint locations
across the meadow of mouthwash blue
water scouted two months prior
by the developer with GPS

WERE-WOLF : MAN-WOLF :: *ELD* AGE : OLD AGE

artificial archipelago
of terraformed resort-sized islets
circled by 386
million tons of breakwater
rocks dropped one
by one
by a dinosaur
crane, huge alien
splash to expose a cluster of sea squirts
splash to quicken the idiot fish
splash to keep the perpetually disconsolate

constitution of the ocean
at a measurable distance
so development can take shape
in peace, can take peace
in the shape of each subsequent installment,
each continent formed
in crude miniature, so when zoomed in on
from the astral vantage
of Google Earth, the project resembles
an atlas of The World
rendered semantically
as luxury
rendered physically
as white sand rising
from the hieratic message of tides

WERE + *ELD* : WORLD :: WORLD : *AGE OF MAN* + EARTH

contractual arrangements kept simple,
the Purchaser enters
into agreement with The World
(deposit required)
provides corporate profile
& construction proposal
(e.g. 64 low-slung bungalows
for the discriminating few hewn
into private cove carved
into contiguous plot of coastline and water
extending to property line
at utility easement, mini marina
with private yacht dock leading
to tiki bar with low-wattage lighting

for Mai Tais and live parrots, oversized
Turkish bathrobes, Egyptian sheets,
infinity pool disappearing into evening
to give the appearance of being
at sea without being
at sea, et cetera)
The World issues final directive
(penultimate payment required)
Purchaser auctions portions to investors
in escrow system,
The World posts island handover date,
Purchaser begins construction,
The World withdraws
to a function of oversight and control

LANGUAGE OF *THE WORLD* : MUTE EARTH :: LANGUAGE OF MAN : MUTE MAN

in the speculation of sheiks & moguls
the portion of The World representing America
goes first, the government of
Ireland buys Ireland, Southeast Asia
remains on the market due to error of depiction
left uncorrected, all of Africa
is still for sale,
the only island / water combo
of the Middle East still up for grabs
is Dubai itself, for to buy
this plot is to buy The World
in the territorial waters just off its coast
and the one within that, and the one
which it is within

A MIGRATING VIRGINIA

A migrating Virginia
possum with frostbite,

      having lost his ears

            and tail, will,

            by definition, fail

            to hear you implore

      get the hell

         out of the upper

         peninsula of Michigan,

but first,

    depending on your version,

          a swan rapes a queen

          or an eagle rapes a virgin

boy and Western Thought

            proceeds from symmetrical

         schemas of violence

           leaking from androgynous

    golden eggs. On condition

    of anonymity, *the secret*

        to longevity

        is staying alive,

             but the blunt

    inertia of civilization

no longer accommodates

        any excess of the ordinary

        and a lagoon of sewage

in Gaza hemorrhages

the retaining wall, a wave of human

        waste chest high

                assumes Umm Al Nasser as

    steel pipe and welding

        machines are banned and

        the ghost of a shepherd

        has burgled the pvc.

EVERY CROP A BUMPER CROP EVERY CROP A BUMPER
SWING A CENSER OVER THE TOMATO SWING A CENSER
OVER THE CROP THE MORE THE MERRIER THE MORE
THE TOMATO TO AUGUR A FISH GENE UP THROUGH THE
STEM TO AUGUR A FISH GENE UP THROUGH THE
MERRIER BLESS THE CONCRETE CLOVERLEAF OVERPASS
WITH FLAMING COCONUT SHELLS ON A STRING BLESS
THE CONCRETE CLOVERLEAF OVERPASS WITH FLAMING
GENE UP THROUGH THE STEM IT'S NEWS YOU CAN USE
IT'S NEWS YOU CAN INJECT THE EMBRYOS WITH
FLUORESCENT GREEN PROTEIN INJECT THE EMBRYOS
WITH FLUORESCENT GREEN NEWS YOU CAN RAISE
HANDFULS OF GRAIN TO THE SKY FOR RAIN OR RAISE
HANDFULS OF PIGLETS TO ULTRAVIOLET LIGHT THE
MORE THE MERRIER THE MORE THE SNOUTS AND
TROTTERS AND TONGUES GLOW GREEN FORGET THE
SEASON FORGET THE GREEN HOWEVER YOU SLICE IT
THE GESTURE'S THE SAME

RED TIDE

Do not endear your eyes
to a cattle egret poised
> in the parking lot
> of the officers' club

at the beachfront Air Force base
> mistaking the hood
> of a Nissan Altima
>> for an ox's spine.

> An ecstatic
>> form of the scenic
> is the obscene.
>> Plovers

>> running the slow advance
> and retreat of surf
>> in ATV tracks

as dune-high satellite
dishes in moonlight glow white as
> moons.
> The scale of naming
> has lost all innocence

> and one of us
> is about to die inside the other.

84

Day workers
night fishing

with turkey liver for snook
stuff snapped lines into

a monofilament disposal bin
until a godhead of nylon peers

out over the pier toward:

1) the city

where the cult of the beautiful has been undone
by the cult of the undone;

2) the ocean

where phytoplankton undergo
a pornographic explosion,

twenty million cells
per liter of seawater.

The traces of idiocy
in each of us,
when proliferated
to the extreme, defeat

intelligence.
Under breakers
odorless neurotoxins

                                    release in the ruptured
                                    algal bloom. If I were an officer

                        I'd be drunk and outranked,
            cataleptic with music

            and spores to the lungs,
                        would cough and choke on

                                            a manner of haunting the air

        while an egret glides
                        toward the windshield of a colonel's
                        Jeep Grand Cherokee.

THE NEW ATLAS

A cartographer enters and endures
pain at the unruled page

To rest the head a moment
against the premise the world

is divisible by two

The coarse sigh of graphite
traveling the ruler's edge

White from white he divides

tree from sycamore
turtle from animal

one from legion
weather from wind

Above the mar: the shape
of a dog; below: the flaw

in the gait of the actual
German shepherd bounding

across the park he is trying to remake
across the pain of the unruled page

Always this, a test
to divide nearness itself

from things that are near

To rest the head a moment
against the endeavor of reflection

Draws a pond, carousel, birch

Write this. To travel from chirp
of bird to chirp of digital

camera, and finding
the second wanting, return

is to have refused
is to have moved

Crept like a convict
one with conviction

across the graphite trench
Grass encroaches on edges

He names a region *The Future*
Lost men wander the arc of its r

Name this. Flies rise in coils

and finding the fog wanting
return to soil

A lost man rests his head a moment
against the sky

My god all I need is a map

The cartographer rolls his premise
into a ring

Slides it into a cylinder

My god all I have are these maps

OBSERVATION

I was longing

        to look at a star

               longer than I have
               ever looked,

went through

        night thistle,

        fire pit,

        waded to

               the sand bar

               in a pond,

               where I found

the bones of an oar

           and the star I was
           looking for,

                  looked long

enough to perceive
the star move

           in low Earth orbit

                  and then I knew
                  I was no longer

looking at a star,

       the star was

           looking at me.

BREAKDOWN COVER

If a man digs a pit, he will fall into it; he remembers that we are dust; little by little makes it grow; on good soil is the one who hears; she may be able to stand her ground; and the earth is a footstool; let all the earth be silent; on earth and under the earth; from the dust of the ground; the earth will wear out like a garment, and whatever you bind on earth will be bound.

Eight states later I enter   the sinkhole plain. An eyeless cave
cricket translucent loses his cling   and jackknifes past alcove,
rubble flow, centuries of limestone   to the depths of the present,
cool echo unbound at the center of it.   I want to grow miserably unused
to my position in history, back up   the stainless steel staircase one
incautious step through time   at a time, lemon wedges
on my eyes, all elbows and ass   between the handrails like a myth
gone wrong, the way   a dream or a wind can be
not bad, but just   *wrong*, incorrect as the airlock
issuing me back into   Kentucky's succor of leaves,
kudzu hemorrhaging   in a triage of trees. A topiary in green
wakes up in limbs, shaggy   mastodons of vines
lumber toward the car   I can't seem to find,
viridian pigeons suspended   between cypresses, wings in various
states of disease. The key   to the four-door
sticks, a man unused   to the monotonous walks
through my chest to plant   in inkjet flyer for
BUCKSNORT.COM on the wiper.   From scoops in the pecans
a green nose appears, distorts   in a gust. Features return time
and again in a head, its slow nod,   as if agreeing the need for tradition
and the need for tradition   to be smashed are one.

HOT POTATO WITH THE NOD

Music. From a box of solid hickory a slow nod is produced and placed upon a girl's shoulders. Her head tilts slightly forward in agreement. Music. She tosses the nod at her father, which drops the man's eyes and neck. Music. The father volleys the nod to his grandfather, inveterate gambler, fisherman, fop. It lands as an incline to the upper torso. Music. The fisherman lobs the inclination toward elders pottering about the commons. Women and men bob up and down at the waist in deference to each other like wooden pecking hens. Music. The eldest straightens and hurls the bowing gesture at her ancestor, a parishioner, who is

94

knocked to his hands and knees before an altar in reverence. Music. The parishioner shoves the bow toward the congregation. The music stops. Hundreds of believers lie face-flat on the floor.

A country founded on simple victuals.
gluttonous. Spare ribs in spare moments.
a wet nap. Pig ears poke through
trailer behind a Kenworth rig,
capable of *fly things* until
empathy. Arc of the meat cleaver,
from dinner. Green beans, baked
cup of slaw, mac & cheese, common
hours slow roasting in the pit,
base-coated by molasses
charcoal debate is the collective
submitting to electronic assistance
at a picnic table, portions mashed
system on Styrofoam, as if dish, course,
intervening fork. A girl squats in weeds
Grease trucks post up in parking
of ways to manipulate heterogeneity
over the speed limit the tilled rows
Chinese fans, the rest a matter of forms
NASA blows up a craft with a comet,
a dirty snowball, the ribbon of raspberry
inching down the boy's chin belongs

Dupe the natives and make a holiday
Every mouth deserves
the air holes of a transport
hogs experiencing *hog things* and flies
a fly drones into a hog ear, auguring
dividing lunch
beans, Texas Toast, paper
denominator of eighteen
dry rub or slop sauce
and honey. Beyond the great gas versus
obsolescence of the old timers,
in the pit. I drip with it
borderless into a holistic
or class would end with an
behind a Winnebago.
lots, lots
into a temporal landscape. At ten
pass like infinitely opening
in the epilepsy of chance.
a comet essentially
SNO-BALL syrup
nowhere else.

BAKED BEAN

Slides up the esophagus, across the expanse of the tongue to the fork tong, lowers to a partitioned plastic plate, cools, rises in a withdrawn waterfall into an overturned tin can, darkens as the circumference seals under an opener backing out, backing down to soil, to the germinating seed, backing up to a planting practice slipping from progeny to progenitor in an unspoken emotion, the toss of a flame beneath a bean softening in maple syrup and bear fat in an earthenware pot on the plain as a horseless man in breeches approaches with a pistol and a song.

Speedometer, moisture-wracked   headlight, head-
rest, armrest, AC, all   dodgy, albeit, and thankfully,
at different times. They jack   the body to probe and tonight
all over the universe porn   stars are sleeping
snug under comforters.   The manager at Chevron sets down
her pen, says only dudes   buy the lemon-hinted water
like it's extreme water,   X-water. Lug nuts
spinzip into place,   I swan dive into amber
viscosity down a funnel   as the X of the X-water lifts
and triples for men   browsing skin in the Lion's Den
Adult Superstore next door.   Position, submission, feats
of flexibility across the offerings,   the free and unregulated flow, no
decision is the wrong decision in case   after case, a cascade of boxes
emptying into multitudinous lust, *née*   luxury until the body loses
the ability to discern even what it's into.   Damn. Each decision
the wrong decision, the body opts   instead for the pattern
in the purple carpet and the hereness   of the warehouse's
cement block wall, exits empty   through theft
sirens into darkness.

Modular

In a remote facility, before demand, the living room travels the line, workstation to workstation, gaining capacity to house memory, picks up a veneer, under clinical light, a closet partition, the arms the hands, the master bedroom, sink and soffit, inspectors' eyes, rafters slapped on with gusset plates, glue to the joints, the arms the hands, conveyed to the flatbed, rolled out the door.

Next to the exit a roller rink	has been demolished,
checkerboard floor left intact,	now slicked with rain.
I encroach from the weeds	to the west,
walk the squares,	reenacting the century's
great game of chess:	Queen to h2 move
a rifle erected in the dust,	a reservist's helmet
hanging on its bayonet.	They bleed the oil line dry
as prefab modular homes	on oversized loads whiz by.
The age demanded redemption	in the quotidian,
but above the hydraulic column	and martyred car,
the fly paper punctuates itself	with black full stops
straining for life against the glue,	and left to the exit,
right to the waiting room,	what's visible & sustainable,
acre after acre,	are contradiction
and decrepitude	gangbanging nostalgia.

Headlight

The berm glows and unglows to its own hazardous heartbeat. Tensile concentration snaps and the high beam retracts its commitment to what sits ahead. Wave recalling particle, beam recanting wave, bulb swallowing beam, system swallowing bulb. High intensity discharge system regresses into a previous incarnation, halogen lumens draw back into the development of lens over filter and filament, regress into fog lamp, into a dimmer pedal operated by a callused foot, decouple from the electrical ignition system, draw down into acetylene flame burning above the bumper as the inventor draws in his formal black frock, moves toward the crowd and unveils, "Gentlemen, a new fire resistant to wind and rain."

Between the voodoomonger   and a troupe of backflippers
backflipping down Beale Street   for cash a frat pack
with collars flipped up   for effect suck
BIG ASS BEER from yellow   mop buckets and harass
the preacher perched atop a step   ladder bellowing a bullhorn
full of sins into the sloshed   face of Memphis. A coin scores
a nod from a man who works   harder than most & predominantly
at pushups, preach's sandwich   board declaims a devotion
to fear, a box of squibs   explodes on the sidewalk
and couples scatter   at the prospect of terror
like horses from a ceremonial   shotgun blast.
The parade's dregs accumulate   in wax cups & elephant
ears left to listen to grass.   Through the chorus of car doors
preach stands unwavering, delivering   big sin, mini sin, sin of the crabapple
and crape myrtle, preventive sin, soft sin,   sin of the devil and the grace until
a hand rests on your shoulder and you   follow it to a man with an aquiline nose
who leans in and whispers, *brother,*   *I know where you got them shoes.*

VERTICES

The index finger approaches the thumb. The bee's vector over the soybean field anticipates collision with a sedan. It is not the thumb that touches, nor is it the finger, but there is touch. For the bee there is no car. The river of machinery flowing in the distance is no traffic, no metal, has no blue-green, is 440 nanometers of disinterested wavelength impressed on compound lenses, progressing. A driver touches his fingers together, apart, together. For him there is no bee, no flight. At best a flicker in periphery, a pointillist daub assumed into the grand idea of field.

Heat index over Dixieland Taxidermy
maxes out at over a hundo
as the sun breaks like an egg yolk
over the hour before dusk.
Through the moving permission
of the open window
a bumblebee crashes into my cheek.
A droplet stretches from a faucet
until the gravity aspect and the circular
aspect crash into it
producing a clear sphere that makes
for the ground. My forearm
slung out the window's gone
brown, rejecting the rest of symmetry
while severed hooves aggregate
on wall-mounted wood
until able to support
the weapons that ended them.
Inadvertent collaborations
amount to the evening, amount
to the curve, a flame like Liberty's
burns excess chemical emissions
off the refinery's stack so the north
side of the byway's a hazard
asymmetrically with the south.
I park and suck
down a bottle of Ozarka.
Genuflect. Sweat. The sun's discus
plants in the horizon.
There is a horrid shape in mind
and if it can be said
to be symmetrical over the line
drawn through dusk,
it is because no matter how I alter
the position from which
I consider it, an aspect remains
the same. Wheel bearings sing
below the manufactured works
and if they can be said
to be symmetrical through time
with other constructions,
regardless of the purposes
we set them to in the present,
it is because of the dead
who live in what we are given,
if what we are given
can be said.

PAIR OF HOOVES

One began as a front hoof and one began as a rear hoof. As a remedy they were coated in a baking-soda-and-water paste and placed in a plastic bag, frozen overnight. In the morning they were both front hooves, but one was larger than the other. As a remedy they were submerged in isopropyl alcohol and exposed to intense UV rays. They then rivaled each other in size, but one was darker. As a remedy, they were massaged with tea tree and lavender oils. Both attained the color of rust, but then one hoof was to the right of the other, and one hoof was to the left of the other. As a remedy, they were dunked in a bath with a ratio of 10:1 water-to-bleach. They surfaced with a newfound contiguousness, but then one hoof was a deer hoof and one hoof was an ox hoof. As a remedy they were laced with daisies between their Vs and sent down the river. When they arrived, they belonged to the same animal, but one hoof was living and one hoof was dead. And they smelled of the living and of the dead. As a remedy, a toothbrush was used to scrub and scrub until the living one bled and the dead one twitched, both in occlusion to "the nothing that is."

Down in the Gulf, Tropical Storm Cindy wiggles her ovipositor
but refuses to lay the hurricane eggs, gets demoted
to a form of depression. I'm bunkered in a pup tent,
tonight's hotter than my hibachi, fat mosquitoes faster
than the laptop. Jackson got a new mayor today
and the residents hit Sears for deals, Sportclips
in the Metrocenter Mall sports a flat screen for dudes.
High performance haircuts, extreme water, X-water.
I pour Ozarka on a toothbrush and sunsets have come
to mean the birth of wolves. One of Noah's hawks escaped
the ark, I met him tonight atop the sagging limbs of the dead
straight pine at Magnum Mound as I walked upon
the prehistoric Plaquemine. I make a pumpkin
trumpet with a buck knife and honk myself
a butchered ballad to break the puberty of silence.
The end of the Trace was the end of civilization, the wilderness
began with an onrush of wind through trees seeming an ocean
or stream in the leaves. As Noah fidgets with the jib sail
in his aqueous tomb in the Ararat of mind, his deranged hawk attacks
the tent for a rasher of beef jerky and even
the shadows are plangent, tearing at one another,
the talons they mimic shredding the nylon while underground
the little metacarpals of a chief's babies sacrificed
to stave off patriarchy rattle on their strings.

A horse is a vain hope for deliverance; the vision pertains to the days yet future; in the past was written to each of us; there is a future for a man of peace; there is knowledge in the past, it will pass; they came forward and carried them; startled and bent forward; they will go and fall backwards, be injured and snared; for our backsliding is great; fell backwards off his chair; his livestock ahead of him; ahead and bowed down to the ground seven times; a hornet ahead; in a pillar of cloud; work he had been doing; where his tent had been earlier; you have been set apart; and the owner has been warned; today or tomorrow we will go to this or that city; with a quota of bricks yesterday or today, as before; the grass withers and the flowers fall; who can add a single hour; a man's life does not consist; keep watch over the door of my lips; yesterday at the seventh hour; to royal position for such a time; to him for a time, times and half a time.

In a pillar of fire to give them light; fire on the altar must be kept burning; and his tongue is a consuming fire; my word like fire declares; you with the spirit and the fire; in the eternal fire prepared; where the fire never goes out; set on fire by a small spark; the elements will be destroyed by fire; snatch others from the fire; the lake of fire is the second death; but only as one escaping through the flames.

The acres-long mound of manure   has been aflame for days,
an infernal caterpillar self-   immolating among bulbous
hay bales — tater tots, oppositely,   photographed from the crop
duster droning in metronomic swoops   over the methane flames.
There's the way a random handshake falls   away from things, away
from a cigarette lighter and a mason jar,   away like a gyre of irrational
consequences from rational decisions,   away now from the one supine
on the stoop perfecting his French   exhale, smoky ribbons
fulgurating from chapped   and slightly parted lips into rotund
nostrils, his knuckles lent   to the nose of an approaching dog.
There's the delicacy   with which he folds palm leaves
into floral shapes to hawk   for three bucks a pop,
how he undresses a tangerine,   notes the ridiculous orange
cones securing the perimeter,   rolling tobacco in pages of the Bible.

In Concert

Everyone I have ever known has given a slow hand to a new dog for the introductory sniff. If I and everyone I have ever known held our palms out to the new dog in concert, just once, we would produce a dramatically common new commitment to timidity. That, or we'd be brutally arranged, pen of zombies, shoal of fish, the safety of staggered movements gone up in a flute of smoke.

Never trust a man who doesn't   *lie or drink.* The bartender in King's
Tavern fiddles with the tassels   on her boingy Fourth of July
antennae. *What sort of animal*   *do you want to be, son?*
The mast of shot glasses   in the sink basin is the colophon
to a dramatic happy hour,   each shot a signal flare
from deep in the tedium soup.   We are a glorious people
rendered in cardboard,   smiling from stools. Judges-at-large

for the annual floozie   contest at the restored saloon

at the water's edge re-mortgage   their relevance with pre-pageant

drivel. *I want to be a bourbon neat*   *sort of animal, ma'am.* Criterion

number one is historical   accuracy. Kitchen's shut

but she will microwave   up some jambalaya if I will

give her *one good reason*   *a chicken's got wings.*

One Becoming

In section XII of The Terrible Vengeance: *"But as soon as night descends and darkness falls, he becomes visible again and is reflected in the lakes and, quivering, his shadow gallops after him." A pale hand turns the page, the word* becomes *is smothered by others, slips, an odorless gas into the memory of a boy who years later scribbles the lyric "What have I become?" on a legal pad, has a hit, gets covered by one of the greats, the word no longer his, dispersed into sixteen-bit pulse-code modulation on a pure polycarbonate plastic compact disc, trucked south from the distribution center, slipped into the machine, lifted, spun through the wire, careening toward the speaker.*

She points her remote   at the omnibus jukebox like a wand

and Johnny Cash drawls   *What have I become?* In the corner

a vet drops a quarter   into the vintage pachinko machine,

each marble becomes its own   foregone conclusion two

thirds of the way through   the forest of pegs. Judges-at-large

lament the loss of Nelly's, the last   operational house of leisure on the river,

how Mr. PCP came & made a scene & with   kerosene, Zippo flicked,

how Nelly made it be he languished   in ICU for weeks, the need

to barricade the hospital to keep   citizens from the windows, from snapping

his neck like a string bean for casserole.

THE MARBLES

In all philosophies of consequence a small glass marble is hosted by a vast glass sphere. The enormity of the circumference of the sphere lends its curved surface a seeming flatness, the marble upon it poised and still. Stillness will never suffice for a host; the sphere begins to spin. A point of touch is a point of reversal. The marble, in smallness, rolls backwards faster to stay in place, a planetary gear. Rolls back past use to its constitution as glass, past its glass to a vial, lightbulb, window. Rolls back through float glass, gem-cutter, conquest. To a furnace, to a blower, to rotational motion at the end of the molten spin. Rolls through heat treatment, transition temperature, an arguable phase. Through liquid, near solid, wineglass, torture instrument, vase. Rolls back to a smear of blood on crystalline silica at the edge of the water. Phoenicians in rows, the docked ship swaying. Nitrum melting in fire beneath pots, their accident a river of futurity flowing from sand.

Two Blue Moons, one fried hard
columnist's abuse of the semicolon
horoscope confirms the quest
pursued thus far will end this
by a bus. Inchoate motion churns
in a manicured hand playing piano
and collects next in a yellow
pennant over the taps,
a beer pong rematch.
speeching for class president,
to depth perception and the sprain
feel them new with each inertial
I settle up, bolt, order
and cheese ciabatta burger
Another twenty-eight-dollar
room means the smoke

catfish po-boy and a sophomore
into it in a frat boy joint my
for *active emptiness, an emptiness center*
month, about the time I get creamed
in this 3-D rebus, settles a moment
on the small of a tattooed back, retracts
point guard stitched into the purple felt
veers off and causes
dank = weed these days, everybody's stump
I want to grow miserably unused
in the state's ankle,
step forward into the assumed.
a Jack in the Box bacon
and a stretch in the undoing.
motel room, sometimes the smoking
alarm's been ripped off the wall.

The receptionist sobs as I slouch   toward a cloud of electrons
posing as a phone, hangs up,   *sorry, I have a daughter*
who hates me. Vacancy. This month   I'll be under a bus, she'll stick
her tongue on her daughter's   nine-volt battery of insults, get shocked,
I'll swallow a contact lens while   looking for the solution, tool
around in trunks, pass a constable   in a cowboy hat as a sorry bird
pecks maniacally at REPENT   stenciled in red on the telephone pole.

JACK IN THE BOX

A large cardboard bin brims with small cardboard boxes, blocks an exit. Most motels are mostly air. What keeps what within? Go for a dip. An hour later entrapment is found broken down, bound in twine beside the ice machine. Like a bulging cardboard folio. Or a prisoner. Chaise after chaise and strips of plastic to elevate wet bodies. It's not the prison bars, it's the space between them. The neat choir of backlit bottles in the bar are mostly air. So is snow. One wall, set in the desert, without the agreement of a second partition to lean on, will always, of its own accord, fall.

Follow the pitchfork   into loose hay,
follow the needle   into the soft infinity
in back of the knee,   follow the headlights'
glowing dowels   into the closet of night
where scrambled trunks rise   from Seven Devils' Swamp
like an aggressive font.   Follow the bicycle
suspended in the tree   as a dollop of gator eye
surfaces, slides, recedes.   Branching neural branching
vascular, being in the trees   reframes what they define.
Muck tucks into corners,   moss drips from limbs.
Ash moss, hair of the wretch,   death stars
in a daisy chain, call it   underwater smoke.

Follow the body to the soup   where divisions fail

in a hail of crickets,   water system soil

system root system blood,   green system reflective system

hidden system blood.   For a definition of fear,

follow the skeptic   into his dissection,

follow his blade   into the ribcage of trees,

follow his doubting finger   into the warm incision,

for if the discharged swamp   exceeds the given

limits of the chest,   gushes in pure freedom,

so it exceeds the security   that the limits to being

a chest provide.

BICYCLES AND TREES

The question was an oak tree destroying itself. And the answer was an acorn. Then the question was the acorn destroying itself. And the answer was another oak tree. In a field of endless green. Then the question was the right pedal coming up. And the answer was the left pedal going down. Then the question was the left pedal coming up. And the answer was the bicycle gliding through lunchtime toward the oak and the oak gliding through lifetimes toward nothing. In a field of endless green. Then the bike collided with the tree, and the oak was destroyed, and the bike was destroyed, and the pedals were scattered, and the trunk had a gash. Thus began the discussion. In a field of endless green. Some were collecting reflectors and acorns. Some were dismayed at the pause. One found the answer to be progression, but what was the damaging question?

Beads from trees, trees a road   dome, beads from phone

wires. Gumbo. Riverboat   casinos ply the current, beads down

strings, the day spelled out   variously in objects and sidewalk chalk.

The things of a place, strung   into an idea of a place,

then rethread to confirm   the idea they've been made to make.

A martial formation of buses   pregnant with eighth graders making

successive lefts to the semaphore
and two breaths ambrosial
sex no strings. The tense
out cowboy boot salesman
Garden hoses coiled by a wort
Waiting for her call the t of today
in copper wire causing the cordless
frozen into trapezoidal funnel
halfway to completion.
on a boy's lost shoe
A snake of four-wheeler
cutting a radial path
After a brutal facemask,
a second string quarterback
wound fast with spinnerets
ascending its string to the beam.
the I out of is toward the am.
procession at an intersection

of a traffic cop. A two-step
with whiskey becoming casual
and tension shift of a strung
as he roasts cocaine on a spoon.
bucket of brew in the basement.
meeting the s of his yes
to string. Portrait of a basketball net
and the basketball arrested
The r from a shoestring
waking the wasp to sting him on the sock.
headlights at night
toward the center of a crater.
a bench-clearer, ejections, suspensions
getting the start. The sac of spider eggs
mislaid in a sow's eye and the spider
The n out of no toward the now,
A woman in the rear of a funeral
floating through the g of green and gone.

THE INTERSECTION

Dozens of watches, yards of linen, tons of iron. Nowhere among the 109 current definitions of terror is a rupture in expectation. Permit this hour that the square root of anxiety is a conflation of the ideological with the substantial. Substance (dozens of watches, yards of linen, tons of iron) put to unintended purposes undermines intent, vaporizes history, leaving the moment rather like the sea. A horse-drawn cart rolls to 23 Wall Street. 100 kg of primitive explosives under burlap. Sea of watches, sea of linen, sea of iron. The flowering horse, the lunchtime crowd, cast-iron slugs. When a car is never again just a car, a man is never again just a man. Nor dozens of watches, nor yards of linen, nor tons of iron. The sea.

Afternoon darkens over a fertile field of refrigerators, a plastic
lawnmower atop the mailbox rattles, a sow wades snout
deep in the pond under lightning slashing the gray
loaf of sky. The stars fell out of grace last night
and landed on license plates. SKYNBEV
is no Russian technocrat but a Beverly who digs Skynyrd.
Eager azaleas explode over wet red dirt and the evacuation
alley unfolds ahead, a nerve flow of vehicles driving
the same day the divided interstate in both directions, tantamount
to a withdrawn compliment. PETPALOOZA!,
then Petpalooza cancelled on account of the saw blade
ready to shred the coast. I want to grow miserably unused
to the rupture of seashores, to altars to measurement, unused
to grain of sand vis-à-vis dune, star vis-à-vis plankton, cliff
vis-à-vis runnel, night, basalt, a constellation of sea kayaks
moving through deep sky reflected. Most of life is approaching
coastlines, but arriving means only step over caution tape, take a leak
in the Gulf, turn immediately around. FREE BEER TOMORROW!,
then free beer tomorrow cancelled on account that the sign's
been hanging over Huguley's meat house for decades.
The storm's thick hair drags across an Astrovan, a camera pans
the fender, travels the jam ahead in search of origin, a primary pileup
to blame. Kill the engine. Wait it out.

A PLANE OF CONSISTENCY IN THE EQUIVOCATIONS OF GOD

Come forward, carry your relatives; from that day forward; of those who shrink back and are destroyed; their horde of faces moves forward; they collect captives like sand; then they walked in backwards and covered their faces; bite the horse's heels so that its rider tumbles backwards; go ahead and do it; look straight ahead; ahead of time; I have been commanded; and he has been guilty; ahead in a narrow place where there is no room to turn; water has been put on the seed and a carcass falls; do not boast about tomorrow; we were born only yesterday and know nothing; the same yesterday, today; her uncleanness was in her skirts; she did not consider her future; when I see the blood, I will pass over you; do not dwell on the past; neither present nor the future, nor any powers, neither height nor depth; at the appointed time; my times are carried on the pinions of eagle wings; broad is the road; times and half a time, out of reach.

Neither he who plants nor he who waters is anything; living water will flow out; cast your bread upon the water; even the winds and the waves obey; anyone who gives you a cup of water; whose waves cast up mire and mud; like a spring whose waters never fail; poured out like water; water through the word; but he who doubts is like a wave; broken cisterns that cannot hold; by the blast of nostrils the waters piled up; a flood to destroy the earth and make it corrupt; surging waters stood firm like a wall; deep waters congealed in the heart; and they sank like lead in the waters.

MOBILE!, a textual   talisman scrawled across plywood
nailed over a barber   shop that went belly up
before last year's hurricane   season petered out.
The waitress in J.O. Wintzell's   oyster house across the street
says *baby love* over and over. Echo: in subtly altering and swallowing
my *hello* shouted into yesterday's trees   the deflecting trunk and bark
attained a voice of their own.   I alter and swallow
crab claw, catfish, black bean   and corn salad, key lime
pie of estimable altitude. Visual   echo: through window and distance
the gale and rain slap and berate   the Z and the V of our shortened
because, our shortened love,   until weather and letters unwittingly
bleed and mean *VIZ* together.   They change with each new customer
reading tossed-off truisms   printed below the photo of J.O.'s
fierce 1938 buzz cut and smile   through a slobber-soft cigar. *A Man Begins*
Grinding His Wisdom Teeth   *The First Time He Bites Off*
More Than He Can Chew.   Gut rock. A line through pinging hail
to the motel. I am the scene,   so to speak, of material echo.
I want to grow miserably unused   to inventories of the immediately
available: room III, toenail   clippings brushed off the floral
bedspread, bar of soap in wax paper   advertising the name of another
motel, curtains sewn together,   broken towel bar from whose hollow
body slides a broken crack pipe   onto the sinusoid swells of orange carpet,
a phone call from a breather,   the cartoonish, vainglorious moose
on the pillowcase, smiling,   unaware of the gun
lovingly rendered at its temple   in ballpoint pen.

Feathers of blood elevate from weeds, congeal in a crimson rope, meet the rising projectile, disfigured from penetration, all heat and soot. Rush together to enter the exit wound, undo the wound channel, the terminal ballistics, redo circulation, muscle shear, force dispersion, crush. A gasp. Projectile exits the entry, spins back through line of flight, slides into caliber of cylinder, the barrel delicately rifled like a swizzle stick, rides fire back down the chamber to cordite powder, to hammer, to spark. Humans are categorized like deer-sized game. They offer exposed organs. They walk upright.

Tongue-warm, beam-lit,   with excess chlorine,
the pool steams from within   its circular cedar fence.
I leave my curiosity   on the esplanade, retreat
to enclosure, float on   a kaleidoscopic beach ball
behind the inn, trunks   abandoned to concrete, defeated.
Open torso to fireworks   feting New Orleans,
open to a weightless interface   between water and body,
body and air called   *Tuesday*, air called *night*.
Early magnolia blossoms   erupt over the change house
like the first popcorn   kernels at threshold.
Like all detonations   fireworks defy perspective.
Spherical spokes come   down toward me
languid in water, up at passengers   in the jet above them,
straight at a blanket of teens   to the east.
Zydeco slides between the slats   to remind what lies
beyond sight. The group of dudes   hucking balled-up
jeans back and forth in front   of the Hustler Club
or the man getting a tattoo   — *RUTHY* — across his bicep.
A slow dance in the Funky Pirate,   teeth into muffuletta,
toes into sand. I spout   arcs of water onto the stomach,

resembling a stone   lawn ornament resembling a man
spouting water.   I want to be done with the stone
and the otherman,   close down realities
beyond the immediate fence,   *for this is what I have,*
this is what's available.   Yet press nose to concrete
and tectonic shifts in mortar   and pebble emerge, whole ranges
to navigate, the heroism of ants.   Any given moment
the given world is infinite,   the fence irrelevant. Tiny intelligences
in substance taunt and slip,   rhizome and reform as fireworks persist,
each revealing for a second   the one that came before,
big spiders of smoke   hanging in the air.

CONES

Immanent to the stationary cone of the eye is the reception and clear definition of the approaching parking cone. Immanent to moving through landscape is an equation whose solution is a gently curving line. The line, like a jet in infinite descent, approaches the horizontal axis in perpetuity yet never touches down. When rotated in three dimensions about the axis, this line produces a new, flared cone whose volume is finite and calculable but whose surface area is infinite. The bucket of paint whose paint can never cover its exterior. The mouthful of words capable of filling the pause between body and body like voluminous music yet small as a mole when written on the skin.

Twice the size of Everest   a plug of pure salt peaks through
the scrim tide marsh in six   circumferential miles of pepper-ready topsoil.
Contra-friction the hand cools   out the window as I encroach
on a tollbooth erected on the wrong   side of the road, directed to veer
left and more left by a progressively   tightening funnel of parking cones.
Fork over two bones. Tabasco, founded   on Avery Island by Avery
McIlhenny has developed jalapeño   ice cream, searing pang

trapped in ice. An ice cubed moved
melts, a gratis soft-serve dollop
melts, the relocated snowy egret
at a minnow in the thrush.
into a gross queue of bodies,
through manners, nods, waits for
waits for the tabernacle
according to custom,
law that is no law.

into the cold of the refrigerator
into the hot of tonsils
jabs its question mark neck
My body melts
waits through meridian sun,
wisteria and hybridized camellia,
covered in lush, waits habitually
according to the iron

The Accident Reveals the Substance

The earth expressed itself in trees. A man was the expression of parents, sex, and genes. In rings, in taproots, in fork of branch and slit of leaf, the tree defied the pull of the earth, expressed itself against itself, outward in opposite directions. Out from the shadows of the forest, the man forced portions of earth to express their summer temperaments as corn and beans. To defy the authority of gravity, he then sent architecture into the sky. The tree persisted in its bald desire until contained within it was the tree-on-fire. To express the excellent velocity of his hands, rapidly the man saturated the earth with faster and faster inventions. Persisted in his desire until contained within the car was a pile-up in the river of merging traffic. Derailment latent in every train, collision and collapse in every girder and airplane. To achieve pure speed and the illusion of freedom, the man then developed television. Others tuned in to watch trees burn. The accident became the condition.

With my bumper I've struck
TWIN STAR MOTEL
and this no accident
condition of the eye
grab-ass with the *was*,
bucket, where through ash
leans beyond consequence

incredible Georgias, mistook
for TWIN STAB MOTEL
of motion, but the permanent
and memory, playing as they do
abandoning the rest to the sub-history
and ephemera a woman
toward a lily to sniff, where fire warms

the pear belly of a chimenea
sweatshirts to assemble
inconsequential, as if the sun
its symbolic obligations.
writhing in a deep ditch.
announces the urinal wall,
to familiar spellings of memory,
in periodic tables shorn
I have entered an atrocious sky
for a dog to sense rain and find minutes
become a congress of worms.
like that of a hawk, I'm sandwiched
and a tulip patch down the exit
thinking how the hell'd
get over here, but each
the station to ask myself
to dash and whisper

and hands emerge from hooded
by its hole. All this, as they say, utterly
still shone only to fulfill
Crosses on the hills, wildflowers
Loco wants deep dick!!!
I want to grow miserably unused
to month upon month arranged
of the true volatility of elements.
but can't remember what it means
later that the median's
The shadow of an overpass passes
between a Harley
ramp toward the hatchery
the Honda with Hawaii plates
time I turn down
the time, I glance wrist to rearview
not yet.

The Given World

Moment. Momentum. Movement. The parcel or particle that tips the scale. A spiral of goldfinches takes up in maples. A little league game unfolds below. The moment has a newspaper and the headline reads: SPONTANEOUS COHESION. *I subtract a tree, the median, loose gravel, a finch. Moment. Momentum. Movement. Arms extend in sweeping motions. Subtract the diamond, my elbow, both teams, a cloud. The particle or parcel that tips the scale. Exemption for sun and exemption for grass, caught as they are between general and particular. Moment. Momentum. Movement. Subtract foreground from background, reduce the mound to its free particulars. Not much difference between half and whole, caught as they are in the authority of measures. For a moment, momentum, substance undoes below. I sneeze and again:* SPONTANEOUS COHESION. *It is not enough that the given world is infinite. It is not enough that the given world is available. We didn't account for reincorporation. What parcel or particle can tip the scale.*

Elbow to elbow, with questions   in an eclectically furnished den.
Did the river of blood that ended   as a vermilion continent in the sunken
garden's gunk begin with a wound   and a hand hot with weapon?
Did it wend through the network   of pipes or simply slide
down the spiral staircase banister   in a vanishing bead past the dumb waiter
and across the tiles of the foyer?   Does the docent
actually believe cooler heads   have prevailed over
the immediate age?   Wooden pugilists spar air
in wall pockets, dessert   is ruined by the two-hundred-year-old
china, recovered from a sunken   warship, oozing embedded
sea salt into peach cobbler.   Could someone called Adeleine
really be rattling the chains   of this place? Tonight I tire
of haunted mansion pathology,   find the sodden plot
at the center of town,   fireflies in holding patterns
above my pin-the-tail-on-   the-donkey body spread
among graves, marvel   at how some remembered
to alter their headstones   in defiance of the given world,
those who then to lived   to be ancient,
and those who were dead   before they were born.

OVERPASS

After obsolescence a cassette is ejected from the deck and chucked out the passenger side. Air funnels through the crenellated eyes of the uptake shaft and rewind shaft, which used to cause revolution. Black tape freefalls in parabolas. From below, the sense of being netted by damaged revolutions. My god, there is a song stuck in there. Many songs.

    and then   you crest
  unknowing and it   straightens out, you crest
     the pined   knuckles and the road

tightens like a piano
has rained, all is
in hand, a plateau
ferns, it has
in tune, out of line,
a steady, toneless
rivulets, the water
this process
in it and it is
is a slick black band
whirling in zoetrope,
exceed the car,
exceeded by their purple,
itself, and nothing else,
outward into air
sliding across slate,
available, no need
no cars, you are
unused
your arms, it blooms
at *the purpose that prevails*
to his purpose
in spirit and purpose
white rent, you've detoured
isn't dirt it is
brown it is
yes, a repast of russet
and in its ions and need it
into *the purpose for which*
the inherited

wire and it
for the moment
carpeted in dark
straightened out, all is
the tires hammer
whoosh, there are
pools, exceeds
you are
unmolested, the asphalt
between stills of forest
the tires
wildflowers are
it opens up and *it is*
it opens
like the whisper of chalk
this is it, all is
to steer, there are
for the moment
to the buoyancy it affords
wide and has failed
has failed *according*
has failed *being one*
and this, the lightning-
into the seam and the dirt
brown and nitrous and isn't
this unforced
and raw umber and you're in it
to last, a total collision
it was sent, it incarcerates
prisons and all

their structural
looming therein, it is
burrowed in math, having
into integers for hours,
and the inversion
proliferate, carve
are exceeded and this
cascading out of your
the book, possess
to accelerate
you close
and crest
onto the piano wire and it
doused metal and green
no words for this,
fourth of the green sign,
its miles, the miles are
bangs wet and there
slate rain,
there is no need
left over, no word
no more cars, you pitch
through the rhetoric
below, the green slacks
and you are
negligence of order,
screeching down the cold
like a luge, like the car
only ever been
and the moth is in

integrity, exonerates what was
like surfacing after having
dunked your head
bobbing for integrals
of fractions as the numbers
a starker relief, as the words
feels like new water
stone mouth, you close
no pedals
or brake,
the eyes, the intent
onto a riverbank, rise
has rained, all is
slacks float in water, there are
the slacks are one
the sign squares, exceeds
not, and you have surfaced,
are parallels there, in each hair and in
what quotient of the seam,
to steer, no grammar
for ditch, for wildflower, there are
left and burrow
of history to a coal car
are tucked there
in motion, a circular
steel on steel
coil of your ear
on its crude rails, there has
one great moth,
this tunnel, this car,

above green slacks a movement

designed,

aflutter it careens

per hour under soil

travels around it

with the message

to speak:

one moth

is you,

have been molesting

they were fixed

threatening

already there, you are

the last unique American

a passenger

against the listing,

through the soil

turns about you in its

and you rest

slacks and a moth

covered with pines,

on the thing itself

in recognition, it belongs

and you are

by the road

to the left.

erratic in a movement

the moth is not

at sixty miles

and the tunnel

like a black envelope

no animal is able

there has only ever been

and that moth

and you

the things of your life as if

and you had somewhere

to be, but you are

not driving

circumstance, are not

bracing yourself

you are in flight

and the interval

negligence of purpose

your palms on your green

settles on the knuckles

yet as soon as you focus

and touch it

to history, is gone

directed to continue on

quavering off

The sun and the air were darkened with smoke from the pit of the abyss; foxes have holes and birds of the air have nests but man has no place to rest his head; blown and tossed by every wind; his way is in the whirlwind and the storm; they took him out into the open air; quickly on the wings of the wind; rent the air with shouts; shouting and throwing off cloaks, flinging dust into the air; into the air, and festering boils broke out; lights in the expanse of the sky; they pant for air like jackals; their eyes fail; the air will feed on those who die in the country; do not fight like a man beating the air; get up and rebuke the wind.

COLOPHON

The Spoils was designed at Coffee House Press,
in the historic Grain Belt Brewery's Bottling House near downtown Minneapolis.
The text is set in Caslon.

FUNDER ACKNOWLEDGMENTS

Coffee House Press is an independent nonprofit literary publisher. Our books are made possible through the generous support of grants and gifts from many foundations, corporate giving programs, state and federal support, and through donations from individuals who believe in the transformational power of literature. This book was made possible, in part, through special project grants from the Jerome Foundation, and the National Endowment for the Arts, a federal agency. Coffee House receives major general operating support from the McKnight Foundation, the Bush Foundation, from Target, and from the Minnesota State Arts Board, through an appropriation by the Minnesota State Legislature and from the National Endowment for the Arts. Coffee House also receives support from: an anonymous donor; the Elmer L. and Eleanor J. Andersen Foundation; Bill Berkson; the James L. and Nancy J. Bildner Foundation; the Patrick and Aimee Butler Family Foundation; the Buuck Family Foundation; the law firm of Fredrikson & Byron, PA.; Jennifer Haugh; Anselm Hollo and Jane Dalrymple-Hollo; Jeffrey Hom; Stephen and Isabel Keating; the Kenneth Koch Literary Estate; Seymour Kornblum and Gerry Lauter; the Lenfestey Family Foundation; Ethan J. Litman; Mary McDermid; Rebecca Rand; the law firm of Schwegman, Lundberg, Woessner, PA.; Charles Steffey and Suzannah Martin; Jeffrey Sugerman; the James R. Thorpe Foundation; Stu Wilson and Mel Barker; the Archie D. & Bertha H. Walker Foundation; the Woessner Freeman Family Foundation; the Wood-Rill Foundation; and many other generous individual donors.

To you and our many readers across the country,
we send our thanks for your continuing support.

Good books are brewing at coffeehousepress.org